Pebble® Plus

Working in SPACE

Martha E H Rustad

raintree

a Capstone company — publishers for children

Raintree is an imprint of Capstone Global Library Limited, a company incorporated in England and Wales having its registered office at 264 Banbury Road, Oxford, OX2 7DY – Registered company number: 6695582

www.raintree.co.uk
myorders@raintree.co.uk

Text © Capstone Global Library Limited 2018
The moral rights of the proprietor have been asserted.

ISBN 978 1 4747 5708 9
22 21 20 19 18
10 9 8 7 6 5 4 3 2 1

British Library Cataloguing in Publication Data
A full catalogue record for this book is available from the British Library.

Editorial Credits
Abby Colich, editor; Kyle Grenz, designer; Tracy Cummins, media researcher; Kathy McColley, production specialist

Photo Credits
NASA Multimedia: 19; NASA Image and Video Library; Cover, 5, 7, 9, 11, 13, 15, 17; Shutterstock: Aphelleon, Design Element, d1sk, Back Cover, Design Element, iurii, 21, Zakharchuk, Design Element

Every effort has been made to contact copyright holders of material reproduced in this book. Any omissions will be rectified in subsequent printings if notice is given to the publisher.

All the internet addresses (URLs) given in this book were valid at the time of going to press. However, due to the dynamic nature of the internet, some addresses may have changed, or sites may have changed or ceased to exist since publication. While the author and publisher regret any inconvenience this may cause readers, no responsibility for any such changes can be accepted by either the author or the publisher.

Note to parents and teachers

The An Astronaut's Life set supports science standards related to space. This book describes and illustrates jobs in space. The images support early readers in understanding the text. The repetition of words and phrases helps early readers learn new words. This book also introduces early readers to subject-specific vocabulary words, which are defined in the Glossary section. Early readers may need assistance to read some words and to use the Contents, Glossary, Read more, Websites, Critical thinking questions and Index sections of the book.

Printed and bound in India.

Contents

Space jobs

Think of working at a job.

At this job you grow plants.

You care for mice. You fix machines too.

And you wear a spacesuit!

Astronauts do all of these things and more.

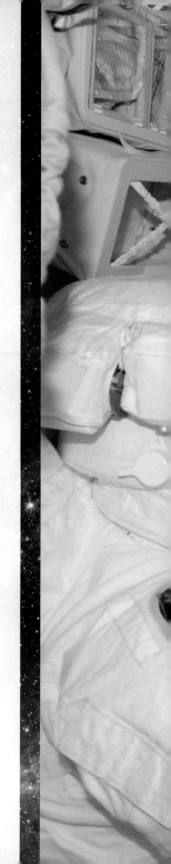

In space everyone has a job.

The commander is in charge of the crew.

Some astronauts are pilots.

They fly the spacecraft.

Other astronauts are in charge of supplies.

Caring for the spacecraft

Astronauts care for all parts of the spacecraft. They fix things that break. They must keep everything clean. Dirt can harm the equipment.

Spacecraft may need repairs

on the outside. Astronauts go on

spacewalks. They wear spacesuits.

Spacesuits keep them safe.

Twist! Turn! They fix the broken parts.

Experiments

Astronauts do experiments. In space, there is less gravity. Less gravity makes living things change. Astronauts study these changes.

Mice, fish and bugs have all
gone to space. Astronauts care for
these animals. They study how
the animals change in space.

Astronauts study plants in space.
They plant seeds. They water
the plants. They may eat food
that they grow.

Astronauts study themselves too!

They may stay in space for a long time.

Their bones grow weaker. Their eyes change.

Studying these changes will help

others to stay safe in space.

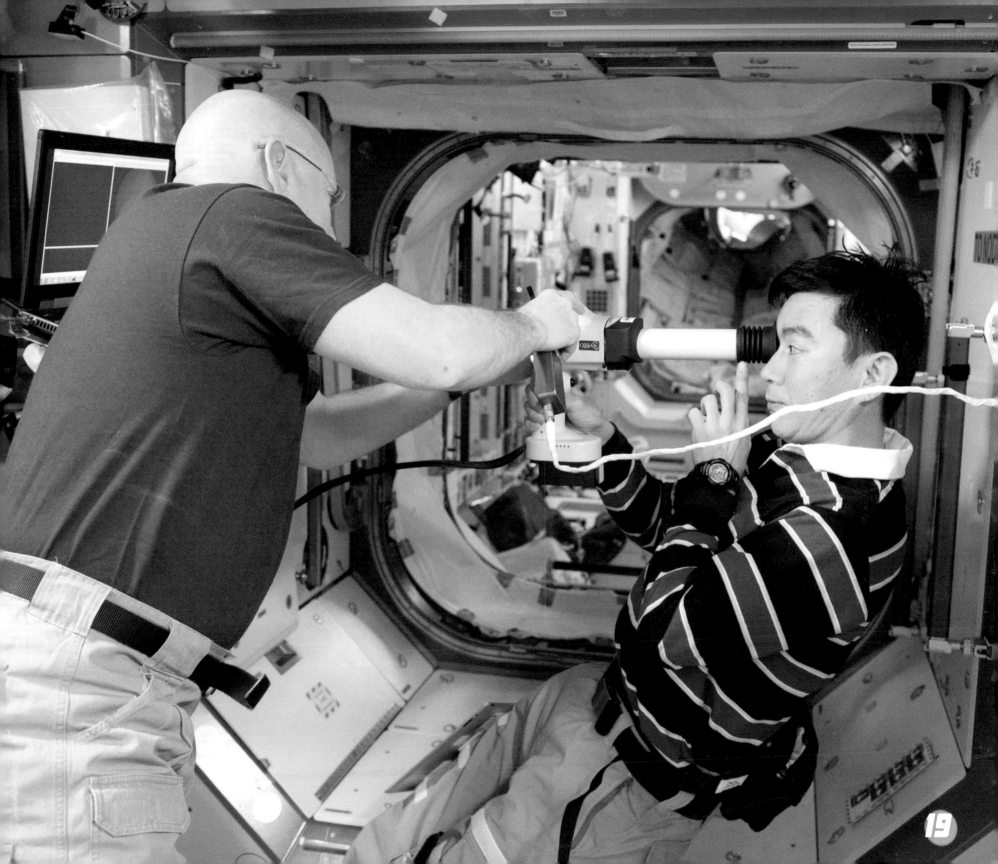

Future jobs in space

Soon astronauts may travel to another planet. They will look for life. Maybe you will have a job in space one day!

GLOSSARY

commander person who leads a group of people

crew team of people who work together

experiment test to find out if something works

gravity force that pulls objects with mass together; gravity pulls objects down towards the centre of Earth

spacesuit suit that keeps an astronaut warm in space

spacewalk period of time during which an astronaut leaves the spacecraft to move around in space

FIND OUT MORE

BOOKS

On the Space Station, Carron Brown and Bee Johnson (Quarto Kids, 2015)

Space Walks (Little Astronauts), Kathryn Clay (Raintree, 2017)

A Visit to a Space Station (Fantasy Field Trips), Claire Throp (Raintree, 2014)

WEBSITES

www.esa.int/esaKIDSen/
European Space Agency for kids

www.bbc.co.uk/education/topics/zkvv4wx
BBC Bitesize Earth and space

www.spacekids.co.uk/spacesuits/
Spacesuits

COMPREHENSION QUESTIONS

1. Name two jobs astronauts can have in space.

2. Reread page 6. Use the glossary on page 22 to find out the meaning of the word "crew."

3. What do you think might happen if an astronaut did not wear a spacesuit during a spacewalk?

INDEX